Designed and produced by Cassell Limited.
35 Red Lion Square, London WC1R 4SG
and at Sydney, Auckland, Toronto, Johannesburg
an affiliate of Macmillan Publishing Co. Inc.
New York

© Darrell Waters Ltd.

Published in the UK by Windward an imprint
owned by W. H. Smith and Son
Registered No 237811 England
Trading as WHS Distributors, Euston Street,
Freemen's Common, Aylestone Road,
Leicester LE2 755

ISBN 0 7112 4930 X

Printed by Morrison and Gibb Limited, Edinburgh

Gulliver's Adventures in the Land of Lilliput

retold by

Enid Blyton

Illustrated by Graham Percy

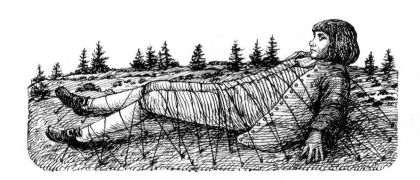

Windward

CONTENTS

I AM CAUGHT BY THE LITTLE MEN

MY NAME is Lemuel Gulliver and I am going to tell you of some of the strange adventures I have had in my life-time.

It happened one day that I was on board ship when a great storm came up. It drove us out of our way, and for some time we had to work so hard that all our men fell ill, and twelve of them died.

Alas, our misfortunes were not at an end, for there suddenly came a thick fog. This closed round us like a blanket, so that we could not see where we were steering. The ship ran on a rock and forthwith split in half.

It became a wreck at once, and the sea came rushing in. I and six other men quickly let down a boat and got in. But a great wave came over us, and the boat sank. My friends sank with it, and I saw no more of them.

I began swimming, and struck out away from the wreck. For a long time I swam, hearing and seeing nothing but the sea. I went on and on, hoping that I should come to land, but seeing none.

Suddenly my feet struck bottom, and I found I was in shallow water, with sand only four or five feet below me. I ceased swimming, and began to walk through the sea. The fog prevented me from seeing the land, and I walked on, the water becoming shallower little by little.

When I had walked a mile I at last came to the shore. I knew I was safe then, and I sank to the ground tired and sad. There I fell fast asleep, and knew nothing for about nine hours.

When I awoke the sun was high in the sky. I remembered where I was, and tried to sit up to look round. But to my great surprise, I could not move even a finger.

There were long, thin cords passed across my chest, and pegged down to the ground on each side. My hands, arms, and legs were pegged in just the same way, and even my long thick hair was made fast to the ground. Although the cord was thin it was very strong, and I could not break it.

A great noise went on around me all this time, but it was not the sound of the sea. I tried to see what made this noise, but I could not, for I was lying flat on my back.

I lay and waited to see what would happen. Presently I felt something creeping up one of my legs. It felt like a little animal of some kind, and I wondered what it was. It walked up my body until it came to my chest, and stood just below my chin.

I looked down and saw, to my very great astonishment, a little man about four or five inches high! He carried a tiny bow and arrows, and beckoned to others like himself. Soon they also came crawling up my body, and stood on my chest.

I could hardly believe my eyes. When I saw all the tiny things stand looking at me I gave a great shout of amazement. This gave them such a fright that they rushed off in fear, and tumbled down from my body to the ground, bumping themselves badly as they did so.

Then after a time, as I lay quiet, they came creeping up again. I could not lie there any longer, so I began pulling at the cords that bound my left arm, and jerked my head to loosen my hair.

Soon I had my arm free, and could turn my head. I tried to catch hold of some of the queer little men, but they ran off shouting in terror.

Then suddenly they flung a crowd of little spears at me, and these stuck in my face and hands like little needles and hurt me very much; I began struggling to get free again, but every time I moved they sent another cloud of spears at me, so that at last I had to stop.

"I will lie still till night," I thought, "and then I will undo the cords with my free left hand, and escape."

Whilst I was thinking this I heard high chattering sounds as if the crowd around me was planning what to do next. Then I heard a knocking by my ear, and discovered that some of the little men were building a sort of platform as high as my head.

It was soon finished, and then I saw four men mount it. One of them spoke to the crowd and immediately some of the midgets ran up and cut away the cords that were still holding my head down.

I could not understand a word that any of them said, and none of them knew what I was saying, but as I was hungry I made signs to them to show them I wanted food. They brought me all sorts of bread and meat and drink.

Everybody watched me eat and drink and was astonished at the amount I swallowed, for to them I was a giant. When I had finished, one of their chief men came and made a speech, and tried to make me understand by signs that I was to be taken to their chief town, not very far away.

They would not unloose me, and they put ointment on my face and hands where the spears had hurt me, and then gave me a drink. There was medicine in it to make me sleep soundly, and soon I knew no more.

I GO TO THE CHIEF TOWN

WHILST I was asleep the little men built a cart to carry me along, for none of theirs was big enough. It was seven feet long, four feet wide, and only three inches from the ground, so it was a queer sort of cart.

When it was made they were puzzled to know how to get me on to it. But they overcame this difficulty by thrusting a great many poles in the ground and putting wheels on the top of them. Cords were run through these and fastened to me. When hundreds of men pulled the other ends of the cords I was gradually lifted off the ground and set on to the cart.

It took them a long time to do this, so they told me afterwards. When they had finished they bound me tightly to the cart in case I should wake, and brought up fifteen hundred of the King's horses to drag me along.

Many men guarded the cart as I was pulled along, fast asleep. I slept until a young man ran his spear up my nose, and tickled it so that I sneezed loudly and woke myself up. This so frightened the crowd of little men on my chest that they ran off in fear, for my sneeze must have sounded like a very loud crash of thunder to them.

All that day we travelled, and half the next. Then we came near the chief town, and the King and all his Court came out to see us. They marvelled at my size, and kept at a safe distance.

I was taken to the one big house in the town, and there I was chained up loosely so that I could walk about. I was even able to stand in front of my house if I wanted to, but could go no further.

Tremendous crowds came to see what I looked like. They stared at me and shouted rude remarks which fortunately I could not understand.

The King and his Court stood on the top of a nearby house and had a good view of me. Later on the King mounted his horse and rode up quite close to me. But the horse shied, and nearly sent the King off his back. When he had calmed the little animal, the King came up and looked at me. He ordered food and drink to be brought to me, and watched me whilst I ate it. Cartloads were brought to me, of course, for their dishes were far too tiny for me to eat from.

After my meal the King and his Court went away, and I was left with the crowd and a few guards. Some of the crowd began to get very rough and rude, and shot at my face so that I was afraid of being blinded.

The guard captured six of these rough men, and bound them up. Then he pushed them to where I could reach them. I did not want to hurt them, but I thought I would give them a fright, so I picked them up and put five of them in my pocket.

The sixth one I held in my hand and pretended I was going to eat him. I took out my knife, and frightened the crowd very much, for they thought I was going to cut off the little man's head.

But instead I cut the cords that bound him and set him down on the ground. He ran off as fast as his legs would carry him! I did the same with all the rest.

I wondered what I should do when bedtime came, for there was certainly no bed big enough for me. To my surprise, the little people brought six hundred of their little beds and put them side by side for me to lie on. But alas! they were so near the ground that my weight bore them down, so that I rested on the hard stone floor.

I lived in the house set apart for me, and as day after day went by I wondered what was going to happen to me.

The King and his Court held meetings to discuss what should be done with me.

"He is a large man," said some, "and he eats so much that soon we shall have no food left."

"He had better be shot, then," said others.

"But what should we do with such a large body?" asked the King.

They were, indeed, very puzzled to know what to do with me. Whilst they were trying to make plans a man told the King how I had set free the six men who had shot at me.

The King was pleased with this, and said he would keep me. He ordered that I was to have as much food as I liked, and servants to wait on me.

"Send out wise men to teach him our language," said the King, "then we shall know more about him."

So I learnt to speak the language, and could soon understand all that was said to me.

One day the King came to see me, and I begged him to set me free.

"If I set you free," he said, "you must swear to do no harm, and you must first be searched in case you have any weapon on you which might harm us."

"Pray search me at once," I said.

So two men were sent to search me. I put them in my pockets one after another, for them to see what I had. Then I took out my possessions and showed them to the King and his Court.

They could not understand my watch at all. They tried to touch the figures and the hands, but the glass prevented them. When they listened to it they said it sounded like a mill working.

They thought my snuff box was a great chest.

"Lift up the lid," said one.

I lifted it up and he jumped into the box! He sank into the snuff, and made it all fly about. Everyone immediately began to sneeze, and I could not help laughing.

No one could guess what my guns were for.

"I will show you what they will do!" I said, and I fired one off.

The noise and smoke frightened everyone so terribly that most of them fell straight down as if they had been shot. Even the King gasped with fear, though he did not fall down, for he was too brave for that.

My guns and my sword were taken away from me, for fear I should use them against the people, but most of the other things were given back to me, and I was very glad of them.

14

THE SIGHTS OF LILLIPUT

AFTER I had been in Lilliput for some time the people became used to me, and although I was a great giant to them, they were no longer afraid of me and I talked to them and they to me, so that I grew to know a great deal about their strange land of Lilliput.

One day I saw a grand show, at which were great crowds, and I saw all the chief men of the land dancing on ropes that were stretched about a foot above the ground. They were very clever at this, and even turned head over heels on the rope. The men who were the cleverest were given the highest posts in the land, which seemed very queer indeed to me.

Another curious thing that I saw the chief men doing, was jumping over or dodging under a stick which the King held either high or low. The one who was quickest at this was given a blue silk thread, the second best was given a red thread, and the third a green. It was indeed very strange to see all the highest men of the land performing such tricks.

One day I had a good idea, and thought I would like to give a show myself for the King to attend. The King said he would come and see it when it was ready.

So I put some poles in the ground, and spread a square of cloth over the top to make a kind of stage. Then I picked up some horsemen and drilled them on the little platform.

The King was so pleased with the show that he came up and sat on the stage himself, while the Queen let me hold her up to see it in her chair. But my show, alas! had to stop, for one of the little horses became fierce, thrust his hoof through the cloth stage, and made a hole.

A thing which the people loved to see was a march past of the King's troops. I used to stand up and put my legs wide apart so that they formed an arch. Then the troops marched through the arch, playing their bands. A very fine sight it was, especially for me, for I had a splendid view of it.

As the weeks passed by I continually asked the King to unchain me and let me go free. At last he agreed.

"But you must promise me that you will not tread on my people," said the King. "And neither must you leave this land unless I say you may. I should be glad, too, if you will help in my battles when I have to fight them."

"I will do all you say," I answered.

So I was set free, and went to see what the town was like. It was quite a strong little place, surrounded by a wall one foot wide and two and a half feet high. I had to take off my coat, for I was afraid the tails might brush against the roofs of the houses and break them, or carry them off.

I went down all their big streets, which were about as wide as a garden path. Their lanes and little streets I could not go down for they were too narrow.

In the middle of the town was the King's house, with a wall so thick that I could not step over it in case I should break it. So I fetched two stools, and, putting one each side of the wall, stepped neatly over.

I lay down on my side and looked in at the windows and saw the King's men moving about in the house. It was a queer sight to me, and one that amused me for some time.

Then I found that it was getting dark and I went back to my house, for I was afraid I might tread on some of the people in the dark and so break my promise to the King.

I HAVE SOME NEW CLOTHES

THE CLOTHES I had on when I came out of the sea had lasted me very well, but they were now showing signs of being worn out. Holes came here and there, and as I had nothing to mend them with I began to be afraid I should soon have to go about in rags.

But luckily before that happened the King said I could have a new suit of clothes made for me. I wondered how that could be managed, but I soon saw that he meant what he said, for he sent his chief tailors to measure me.

"You must kneel down," they said.

So I knelt down, and they placed a ladder against my side. One of them ran up to the top, and dropped a line down from my shoulders to the floor.

"Now we know the length of your coat," they said, and put it down in a note book.

I said I would take the size of my waist and arms myself. So I did, and told them what to put down.

"That is all the figures we shall want," they said. "We can find out all the other measurements by doing sums."

The cloth they made was very small, of course, for they could not weave a large enough piece for me. So they made many many small pieces and joined them all together. My suit fitted me when it was done, but it looked very queer, for it was all in small pieces as if it had been cut out of a patchwork quilt.

I was one day very pleased to get my hat, which I thought I had lost. I had supposed the sea must have swallowed it, and thought no more of it, though I should have been glad of it to keep the sun from my head.

The little men found it on the shore, and could not think what it was. They came running into the town, saying that a great black thing lay on the beach, the like of which they had never seen before.

They said they thought it must belong to me because it was so big. The King said it must be fetched, and sent five of his horses to bring it. Two holes were bored in the brim and cords were put through and tied to the horses. Then they started off and dragged it to the King's town.

"It is my hat!" I cried in delight, and picked it up. I cut the cords and

clapped it on my head. It was very little hurt by the sea or by the dragging it had had along the roads, and I was very glad to see it.

Soon I found it was unpleasant always to have my meals on the floor, so I made myself a strong table and a chair, and asked that I might have my food on the table. As I had plenty of men to wait on me it was not difficult, as the dishes were brought up to me as I wanted them. I used to pick up a dozen men and put them on the table so that they could look after me, and take away the empty dishes.

The King one day sent word that he would like to see me eat. So I determined to show him what I could do in that way, and make him marvel at the amount of food I could swallow.

The King and Queen both came, and I lifted them up on to the table and set their little thrones there too. They sat down in front of me and begged me to begin.

I ate as much as I could, and kept my little servants running all about for dishes here and dishes there. The King was amazed to see how much I ate. Then I picked up the little barrels in which they always put my drink, and drained them off, one after another.

The King and Queen said very little, and left me after I had finished. I hoped they were pleased, but I found out afterwards that they were not, for the King, seeing what a tremendous amount of food I could eat, began to think of the great expense I was, and it displeased him.

He was not so friendly to me after that, and then other things happened, of which I will tell you, which made him still more unfriendly, so that I was beginning to wish I could leave the land of Lilliput, and go back to my own home once more.

I AM ASKED FOR HELP

I HAD not been free very long when a visitor came to have a long talk with me. He was one of the great ones of the land, and came from the King's Court.

He told me many things about Lilliput which I did not know.

"Although you may perhaps think that our land is full of peace," he said, "that is not so at all. There are two sets of men in the country who are bitterly against each other, and would like to do all they could to harm one another. Neither set will do anything to help the other."

"What do these two parties call themselves?" I asked.

"One is called Low Heels, the other is called High Heels," answered the great man. "They are named so because of the difference in their shoes. A Low Heel would scorn to wear high heels, and a High Heel could not bear to be seen in low heels. So you see the bitterness is very great."

I thought this was all very strange, and said so.

"It makes things very difficult," said my visitor, with a sigh. "You see at present all the Low Heels hold the chief places in the land, and are the great ones, but as the High Heels refuse to do anything the Low Heels command them to do, the country is at a standstill, and the State can do nothing. It is a good moment for an enemy to make war on us, for we do not stand together."

"Do you think anyone is going to fight you?" I asked.

"Yes," he answered, "we are afraid that the men of the land of Blefusen are going to send a great fleet against us."

"Why should they do that?" I asked. "What is their quarrel with you?"

"I will tell you," he said. "It all began through breaking eggs at the big end."

At this I was greatly astonished, for it seemed to me to be a poor cause for quarrel. My visitor went on with his story.

"Once upon a time," he said, "all we Lilliputians broke our eggs at the big end. Then one day the King's son accidentally cut his hand through this manner of breaking eggs. The King was very upset, and forthwith issued a proclamation to say that eggs must from that time be broken at the small end."

"This is very interesting," I said.

"Some, however," went on my visitor, "refused to alter their custom, and continued opening their eggs at the big end. The King was angry, and they at last had to fly the country. They went to Blefusen, and told their trouble to the King of that country. He took their part and declared war on Lilliput."

"They are going to send a fleet soon, I think you said?" I asked my visitor.

"We have heard that they have made ready a very large one," said the great man, "and the King desires your help in fighting it. You are so big that you will surely be able to help us defeat it."

"Pray tell the King that I shall be delighted to help him," I said. "I will at once think out a plan."

My visitor went, and I was left alone to think out the best way of fighting a fleet. I knew that the ships would be very small to me, and it was not long before I had thought of an excellent plan.

I asked how deep the sea was round about Blefusen, and found it was only six feet in depth. I was also told how large the fleet was. I then set about putting my plan in practice.

First of all I made a great many iron hooks. Then I fixed these carefully on many strong ropes I had made. After that I went down to the sea with them. I waded out, and swam some little way, and in about half an hour reached the place where the fleet of Blefusen lay at anchor.

When the men of Blefusen saw me coming near they were horrified. They shouted with terror, and fled from all the ships, as I had hoped they would do. The rest of my task was easy.

I took up my hooks and ropes and fixed a hook on the prow of each ship. Then I tied all the ropes together at their other ends, took the knot in my hand and began to pull.

When the enemy saw what I was doing they were furious. They came down to the shore and threw hundreds of spears at me. Some of them stuck into my hands and my face, and I began to be afraid that I should get them in my eyes, and so lose my eyesight.

Suddenly I remembered my eye-glasses, which I had carefully hidden from the King in case he should take them away. I took them out and put them on. Then, with my eyes well protected, I went on with my work.

I pulled the ropes that were fastened to the ships, and the whole fleet began to move. The men of Blefusen sent up a cry of grief and anger when they saw their fleet being pulled away from the shore and taken to Lilliput.

The King of Lilliput and all his Court had been watching from the shore. I had to swim for a little way at first, and they lost sight of me. When they saw the fleet moving, and no sign of me, they were frightened, for they thought I must be dead, and that the fleet was sailing for Lilliput to make war on them.

Then I came to a shallow place, and stood up to walk through the sea, drawing the ships after me. When they saw me the King and his Court cheered and shouted for joy, for they then knew what I had done.

The King gave me a fine welcome, and everyone thought I was a great hero. They were all very kind to me, and the King made me one of his chief men.

One day the King sent for me, and said that, as it had been so easy for me to capture the fleet of Blefusen, he would now like me to go to the enemy's country and take the whole of it for him.

"Then you can make all the folk there break their eggs at the small end, as I have commanded," he said.

"I cannot do that," I said, "for I will not make slaves of any men, even if they be my enemy."

The King was angry at this, and became very displeased with me. He told some of his chief men that I had refused to do what he asked, and as they were jealous of me, they were glad to find the King was angry. They did all they could to make him more and more displeased, thinking that if they could make him hate me I should not be allowed to live in peace and plenty as I had been doing.

One day the King of Blefusen, having lost all his fleet and hopes of winning, sent to say that he would make peace. His messenger visited the King of Lilliput first, and then came to see me.

"The King of Blefusen sends greetings," he said, "and he would be glad to see such a man as you, if you will visit his Court at your pleasure."

"I will certainly come," I said. "Pray thank the King and tell him I will come as soon as I can."

I GO TO BLEFUSEN

I SET off in a few days. In the bay was a large ship. ''This will do well to carry my clothes,'' I said, and drew it to the shore. I piled my things on it, and then waded into the water.

In about half an hour I came to Blefusen. The King and his Queen came to meet me, and all the Court came with them. They marvelled at me, and seemed very glad to see me.

I kissed the hands of the King and Queen, and to do this I had to lie down on the ground. I did not tell them what had brought me to Blefusen, but let them think I was visiting them, as I had said I would. They were all very kind to me, and treated me very well.

I stayed there for some days, seeing the sights of Blefusen, and talking with the King and his Court. Then one day I saw something in the sea which made my heart leap. It was very big—or so it seemed to me after my long stay with the little people—and I knew it must come from one of my own lands. I thought it looked like a boat floating upside down.

I waded into the water, and swam out to it. I found that I was right, and that it was a large boat. I was overjoyed for I at once thought that here was a way of escape from Lilliput and Blefusen, and a way which, with some luck, might take me back to my own country.

I asked the King to let me have some ships to help in pulling the boat to land. With the help of these, and my own strength, I soon pulled the boat in to the shore, and then tried to turn it the right way up.

When that was done I found it was a good boat, and one that I could certainly use to sail away in. I went to the King and told him.

''I wish to get back to my own country,'' I said, ''and this boat will take me, if only I can get oars, sails and masts.''

''We will help you,'' the King said generously. ''It shall be fitted up exactly as you wish.''

I was so pleased that I could hardly wait to begin. I knew I would need a great many things before I could safely start off, and I set to work to make them.

In the midst of this there came a messenger from Lilliput. He had been sent by the King to say I was to go back at once. I was to be bound hand and foot and sent back in that way.

The King of Blefusen laughed and sent back another message.

"Tell your master," he said, "that I cannot bind this man. Tell him, also, that he has found a huge ship, and that he will soon set sail in it, and leave us for his own land."

I went on with my work of fitting up my boat. I made oars and sails, and fine strong masts, and at last the ship was ready, and I determined to set sail in it at once.

The King of Blefusen gave me a great store of food and drink and this I put on board, for I did not know how long I should be in the boat.

"I should like to take some of your people with me," I told the King. "For they would be greatly marvelled at in my own country."

But the King refused to let me take any of them, and begged me not to do so. He told me, however, that I could take some of the animals of Blefusen with me, and I was glad of that, and put many of the tiny creatures on board.

When I was ready to go, the King sent some men to search me, for he was afraid I might take some of his people away with me. But as I did not intend to do so, they found none on me or in my boat.

Then the time came for me to say good-bye to all the little people. I bade the King and his Court farewell, and thanked them for their great kindness to me.

As a parting gift the King gave me some bags of gold, and also his picture, painted at full length. I was very pleased and put them carefully away in one of my gloves, so that they should be safe. Then the last good-byes were said, my boat was pushed away from the shore, and I jumped in and set sail. I saw the Land of Blefusen growing fainter and fainter, and soon lost sight of it altogether.

I set my face to the open sea, and steered by the sun and the stars. I hoped to fall in with a ship sooner or later, and kept a sharp look-out.

All the day I saw none. The stars came out, and I slept, having first eaten some of the food I had stored in my boat. When the sun rose I awoke, and at first wondered where I was. But I soon remembered and was glad to think I was perhaps on my way home.

Once more I sailed on hoping to meet a ship, and again night came without my having done so. But the next day I was more fortunate, and saw a great ship on her way across the sea.

When she came near I hailed her, and she saw me. She took me on board, and her men questioned me as to who I was and where I had come from. I found, to my great delight, that they were going home from a journey to the East, and would willingly take me with them.

I told them of the wreck of my ship, and how I came to the Land of Lilliput.

"The people were only so high," I told them, and showed them what height the Lilliputians stood from the ground. I told them of my strange life there, and how I had captured a whole fleet at once. Then I related how I had gone to Blefusen, and found a boat out at sea, which boat was the one they had just rescued me from.

They all listened to my strange tale, but no one believed a word of it. They thought I was either mad or untruthful.

So I took out the little bags of tiny gold coins, and let them see them, and then I showed them my little animals, all alive and moving.

Then they could do nothing but believe me, they marvelled at my wonderful adventures. They could hardly believe the little beasts were alive, but when they saw them feeding, they had no more doubts.

I sailed with the ship for many months, for we were a long way from home. My little animals all lived, except one which a rat carried off. Nothing was left of it but the bones. All the others throve well.

When I got home my wife was overjoyed to see me, for she had thought me dead. She was amazed to hear of my adventures and much delighted with the little beasts.

I let them graze on a patch of fine grass, and they did very well. So many folks wanted to see them that I charged each one a fee for a visit, and soon I became quite rich with all the gold I saved.

Then one day I sold my sheep for six hundred pounds, and that was the end of them for me.

I soon became used to seeing things their natural size once more, but at first I thought everything looked tremendously big, after having seen tiny things for so long. After a time I settled down, and my wife hoped I would not go to sea any more.

But there came a time when I felt I must go on my travels again, and when I set out I had even more marvellous adventures. Some day I will tell you about them in another book.